Under Glass is a dialogue between a series of prose poems, following a protagonist through a mysterious and threatening landscape, and a series of verse poems, driven by the speaker's compulsive hunger to make sense of things. Gregory Kan's outer and inner landscapes frequently cross paths but leave the reader in doubt – this is a collection full of maps and trapdoors, labyrinths and fragmented traces.

Gregory Kan's work has featured in literary journals such as *Atlanta Review, Cordite, Jacket, Landfall, The Listener, SPORT* and *Best New Zealand Poems*, as well as art exhibitions, journals and catalogues. His first book of poetry, *This Paper Boat*, was shortlisted for the 2017 Ockham New Zealand Book Awards.

UNDER GLASS

GREGORY KAN

AUCKLAND
UNIVERSITY
PRESS

On one side of the river is a colossal jungle, a green so dark it's nearly black, and on the other is a sandy plain patched with tall grass. I follow the river's straight rule towards the coast.

Here, there are two suns. The ordinary sun is in the sky overhead. The other sun is eating its way out from inside me.

I wanted what happened to be something

I could know

and I wanted what I knew to be something

I could describe

something to which others could say

I know this

this happened to me also.

At the back of the room is a mirror

dreaming it's become itself at last.

I keep walking

as if I know all the parts

and could play them.

Today the world overwhelms me.

I feel a garden

growing in my mouth

and eventually touch stone.

I am afraid of appearing sentimental about sentimental things.

The things that are really big and really close

are too big and too close to be seen.

People are supposed to know everything

and when you find out that they don't

it hurts for all time.

I can't see any other feature of the land, just the surrounding trees, and the surrounding water. I don't want to have to sleep here, the banks rotting into mud, the water thick with slime. The land writhes, and I writhe with it.

There are two suns. The second sun is hiding in the submerged roots of a nearby tree, giving me what I can get, the only way I can get it.

You thought that because you had less

you would take everything.

You always think about what you could lose

without really losing anything.

If you live in a mind

that destroys itself

to comfort itself

then I think I can understand

but right now I am tired of understanding.

I thought that the things I loved

were places I could always go back to

but the spaces between things become places themselves

and threaten to swallow me whole.

I thought that knowing in just the right way

would be enough to free me from pain.

For those of us who drowned,

and continue living underwater,

this isn't heaven

but I hope we could come at last to love it.

I wake in the middle of the night. The ground is dry and sandy beneath me. I can hear the waves, even though I can't see them yet. The thick canopy has given way to an expansive sky. For a moment, the moon bleaches everything white, and I am a black arrow stretched across a bright field. I fall asleep again, and dream of a house with many doors.

I fall into the deafness of the second sun and become several outlines of myself.

No matter which outcome

in the dizzying array of all possible futures

no matter the fear

I will meet you there.

I undress and dress

eating my own shadows

until the corridor appears again.

I think about asking if you will cope

which is a stupid question

so instead I ask if you will keep going no matter what.

I feel cruel when I tell you that each day

something we love tries to save us

because sometimes I'm right

and it's what we hope for

but can never quite believe.

Now I am floating towards the trees. Now I am floating among the branches. This is the house. This is the gate. Now I am lying on the floor in one of the rooms, holding a brick above my chest.

I swallow the second sun and the night releases me. I am full of holes in a night full of holes.

When I lurk on the edge of something

it is a way for me to feel close to that thing

without actually touching it.

If I weren't so scared of life

I wouldn't be here

watching the thing inside me

watch your face

to see if anything has changed.

I tell myself it's okay to just sit here

and breathe

over and over.

I taunt myself when I feel dirty with guilt.

I'm too busy stifling my anger to see what's causing it.

I want fixed terms by which to measure my experience.

I must be either high, or dying.

I don't want to know many small things.

I want to know one big fucking thing

and call it either shame, or home.

But this is not a dream, this is the sea. The sea is a house made of anything. The sea is a story about anything, told by someone unfit for storytelling. More than what I can know, and much more than what I can understand.

The second sun is a house made of many doors. I disappear to reappear in many places at once.

Help me understand you without the need for names.

I want to want something

the way you do

and love myself for it

the way you do

and soften against the slow vines of your neck.

You described to me

how after coming

the waves recede from your outstretched hand

and how you're sure then

that we have mass

and impact the bodies around us

even though we don't always know

who we are

where we're headed

or if we're doing any good.

The second sun is falling through me. The sea is on fire, the sand is on fire, the sky is on fire, and the trees are on fire.

One day you turned and we were gone.

The absence was impressive and you lied to us to lie to yourself.

You saw all your fears and wishes

but not why you continued to hoard them.

Some days it feels like you might kill me

for what you think the world owes you

and for everything I tried to give you

that you believed

was just a sign of what I hadn't given.

I still care about what you think of me.

Whatever I say I am to myself

I am moved by the things I can't think clearly

like the so-called trees

and the so-called sky

like my so-called hands strangling the so-called trees

of our shared hurt.

Every day the coast looks the same, as though I haven't moved. The lighthouse is a tiny finger thrust up against the horizon. I am running out of food and water.

The second sun is the immovable neck of the world I pass through just to pass through.

I'm trying to stop doing the thing

that you sometimes complain about

but what I thought I left

I sometimes find again

and sometimes when I go looking for what I thought I had

it isn't there

and so I draw my ideas cruelly around me

which is the power I have

to trap myself within revolving doors.

Sometimes I write so that you can be punished

the way I think I deserve to be punished.

Things don't happen because they mean something

but I have to believe that things can change

and that when they do

we have ways of knowing it.

It's noon by the time I reach the lighthouse. I look at the little window halfway up its swirled black-and-white stem, and then to the windows of the lantern room at the top. I think about the difference between being in a high place and being in a low place.

The second sun is a dark seed in my palm with my fingers closed over it.

I feel like I’m losing time

and that makes me cruel.

Stay with me

because I am just about ready to exist.

I wanted to help you get

to where I selfishly thought you should be

but I wasn’t paying attention

and now I’m trapped on a dinghy somewhere.

A memory of domination

that would find us all years later

as indistinct survivors

all with the same face

all with the same eyes

that would hurl us backwards

with a current so strong

we all knew it was happening

when it was happening

but could not do a thing about it

so strong I still find it hard

to believe it could ever

have happened to us.

The lighthouse has been abandoned for a long time. Inside, I find that the spiral staircase leads down below the ground, as well as to the glass lantern above. I have the feeling that someone was standing in the same place, just a moment before me, one hand holding onto the land, the other filling with sea.

The second sun: I haven't got it. I can't see it. It does nothing for me except draw me on. No fear stands up to it and no patience can wear it out.

It's hard

from the world of all possible things

to choose the things that are actually happening.

You haunt me properly.

Confusing myself is a way to be honest.

Confusing you with something inside me

is a way for me to lie to myself

to tell you the truth

because I am the worst evidence provided

in support of myself.

It’s cold

and we are hurting each other elegantly with our fears.

I am afraid to stay on the earth

with all the holes in my skin.

It seemed like what we touched was ours.

It seemed like what we touched we couldn’t hold.

It seemed like we might just turn and stumble right back in.

We have been so tired and ashamed

that the past could kill us.

The light fixtures have all been removed or broken. I descend the stairs. The first underground level is empty except for a kerosene lamp and the smell of urine.

I recognise the second sun from a distance, but not up close. It carries the incompleteness through which it can be seen.

Moving from one world to another

is like dying in a dream

of hands and water.

Nothing is forgiven because

nothing is remembered

but the desires remain the same:

to be in a room with others

satisfied

tired of wonder

holding each other

with the good secret

of no longer having to insist on going

where we think we have to go.

I’ve grown old

remembering this garden.

Often you didn’t know

that you were happy

and I guess how could you have known, yourself

when I saw you as I did

you who wanted to lose nothing

know nothing

see nothing

just so long as I got to where

you wanted me to be.

Climbing lower still, I find a faded photograph in a broken frame dangling beside the stairwell. The second underground floor is bare except for a few chairs and a rickety table with a rug beneath it. The stairwell ends here. I lower the half-blackened lamp onto the table and search the room.

The second sun is a shiny black window. It eats the surrounding air. It is the only fixed point in a spinning world.

When you move

a look moves inside me

and eats there what I eat.

I think about power

and how it always

insists on itself:

a place from which to speak,

a place from which to look at other people

while also being seen,

a hand opening

towards what seems like forever.

I pull back the rug. A square trapdoor is hidden beneath. Below it are more stairs leading down. Looking up towards the top of the stairwell, I see the gleam of the lighthouse lamp.

The second sun reveals all and remembers nothing. It takes up more room than anything that is actually there.

I survived it happening

but not the shame.

Here is the place where they will keep me.

Here is the place where they will keep me.

Here is the place where they will keep me.

I want to feel like I'm doing something

to feel as I feel comfortable feeling

to seem as I feel comfortable seeming.

I want an open field to taunt with the possibility of my absence.

I don't want my body to turn into something different.

I don't want to leave the place where I live and the people I love

so I turn towards the only thing I know.

The steps continue to lead down, with small rooms or caverns branching off them erratically. I move through a hole from one space to another unexpected space. I follow the sound of bubbling, hoping to find a stream I can drink from.

It makes no sense to think of the second sun as either an open or closed thing. The second sun is a network of cracks in the air, with no discernible beginning or end.

I wonder where you are and what you are doing.

If I were to meet you again

I wonder if you would still insist that you cannot understand

how it's possible for someone to stumble like I did.

There's a room

that we keep finding ourselves in

and in that room

there's a river

and in that river

there's a voice

and in that voice

there's a history of power

that we eat in black mouthfuls

barely coming up for breath.

I start marking the walls with my knife so I know where I've been. I begin to grow disoriented. Here, below the lighthouse, the walls are made of strange stone. Their smoothness and the iridescence that my light draws out of them reminds me of mother-of-pearl.

Everything that surrounds the second sun is not part of it but nonetheless makes it what it is.

I think the beginning of anything

is always a secret.

I love myself when my mind is fucking

the hinges of events.

Each new thing you see

is placed beside every other thing you have ever seen

and when I think about someone

who's seen so many bad things

I can understand why

a good thing can sometimes hardly be believed.

I try to find my way back to the trapdoor, but there are passages leading in every direction. At times the caverns seem larger, and the few things in them further apart. The Persian word for labyrinth, *hezar-tu*, roughly translates as 'a thousand insides', 'a thousand withins'.

I have my worries, I have my names, and I have the second sun. At first I couldn't look, and now I can't look away.

You were punished for doing some things

and punished into doing others

as if they knew just by watching

where you ended

and where everything else began.

You think I don't know you anymore

and I never read your emails

but I wonder if we have the same nightmare

about some final thing

for which there is no forgiveness.

I don't know what kind of place this is, or if this even is a place, and because I don't know if this even is a place, I'm not sure I can ever leave.

There is the ordinary sun and there is the second sun. I break into pieces, and the pieces break into pieces. I walk into the second sun. I become an empty sign.

When real things trouble me

I begin to trust what isn't real

because it helps me

whoever I am

when I make it up

whoever I am

when I am not the sort of person I want to imagine

and because real things continue not to help me.

I go slow

holding back and allowing myself only

to feel around the edges of things

until I can’t

until I have to plunge right in.

The second sun is turning the air silver, and I am turning silver in the air, silver through my clothes, through my eyes. Silver through my teeth.

It’s like you’ve gone very far away

even though you haven’t gone anywhere at all.

I know some questions can destroy us

if we are denied the answers long enough.

I can feel us looping

which is to say

I can feel us imperfectly circling

something we both want

as we stumble more tightly

into each other's arms

and there is time

there is still time.

A narrow tunnel opens up into a space whose limits lie far beyond the glow of my lamp.

I have a tiny black sun on my hot skull.

I don't want this part of me

to touch any other part of me

because it's hard sometimes

to feel continuous

and filthy.

Sometimes when you have your back turned

I have my back turned.

Sometimes when you have your back turned

I turn around

and look at your back.

Sometimes when I turn around and look at your back

you turn around

and then we look at each other.

A giant, mouldering pile of letters and notes reaches the ceiling of the cave. Near the bottom, it's beginning to rot.

The second sun is a vanishing point I lean towards. It is growing at one metre per second.

I know without needing a picture of it –

this place where we are safe enough

to repeat ourselves.

You are tired.

You begin to dream.

You are a field of overlapping surfaces.

It changes your sense of scale

to know you can disintegrate

to forget the difference

between your skin and sinking.

Secret inside a secret,

tonight it is the only door through which

you can be made to disappear.

At first I handle each page with great care, afraid it might dissolve in my hands. At some point, I start to assail the clot of inscriptions more directly, to wade into its fetid belly. I shove my arms into the mess and come out holding whatever my hands can grasp.

I reflect myself in the second sun the world has made of me. I've never known a closeness as alien as this.

We drove all day

without hands, or eyes, or feet.

Urgency is a speed we perfect together.

We drove all day

no hunger to speak of

but to speak with.

I am here.

I can see.

I can choose.

My breath is a rope

and for a while

I tie a knot

and will not let it ease.

It could be a dark window. It could be the diameter of a million or more dreams. It could be the stillness of a world going slowly blind. It could be the only still point in a world that turns blindly. It could be a place I can imagine but that I could never reach. It could be the something outside of everything. It could be that the inside of anything is just as outside as the outside of anything. It could be what I forgot I was holding in my hand.

I want to seem to you

the very same thing that I seem to myself

and I want to seem to myself

the very same thing

that I am

but nothing is honest enough

walking around and around a thing

I do not know, and cannot touch.

I look at your face

and I can't believe how I got here

and how lucky I've been.

I don't want to forget even the smallest part of this.

I don't want even the smallest part of this to be wasted

and I will carry this sensation with me

through all the hard places.

You can always find me.

You said you could feel

everything inside you

everything in this room

everything in your life up to now that made you this way

everything in the feeling of what you meant

gather behind your eyes.

I walk through a crack in the second sun. The second sun does not fill or leak. I continue to walk, dreaming of warmth.

Notes

I sampled and adapted many small moments from the following texts (including my own):

Tusiata Avia, *Fale Aitu | Spirit House*, Victoria University Press, 2016
Mary Burger, *Sonny*, Leon Works, 2005
Mary Burger, *Then Go On*, Litmus Press, 2012
Anne Carson, *Nox*, New Directions, 2010
Lucille Clifton, *The Collected Poems of Lucille Clifton 1965–2010*, BOA Editions, 2012
Clark Coolidge, *The Crystal Text*, Sun & Moon Press, 2000
Dennis Cooper, *The Dream Police: Selected Poems, 1969–1993*, Grove Press, 1996
Joseph Conrad, *Heart of Darkness*, Penguin Classics, 2012
Lydia Davis, *The Collected Stories of Lydia Davis*, Picador, 2010
Jenny Holzer, *Jenny Holzer: Laments* (DIA Art Foundation, NYC 1990), posted by J. Christian Guerrero, 25 December 2012, www.youtube.com/watch?v=UEiJ7GGJtPo
David Joselit, Joan Simon, Renata Salecl & Jenny Holzer, *Jenny Holzer*, Phaidon Press, 1998
Gregory Kan, 'The Act of Observing', *ars viva 2018*, Sternberg Press, 2017
Gregory Kan, *This Paper Boat*, Auckland University Press, 2016
Gregory Kan, 'The Incompleteness of Burning', *grammars*, Dunedin Public Art Gallery, 2016
Courtney Sina Meredith, *Tail of the Taniwha: A Collection of Short Stories*, Beatnik Publishing, 2016
W. S. Merwin, *The Shadow of Sirius*, Copper Canyon Press, 2009
W. S. Merwin, *The Essential*, Copper Canyon Press, 2017
Ariana Reines, *Mercury*, Fence Books, 2011
Rumi, *The Soul of Rumi: A New Collection of Ecstatic Poems*, translated by Coleman Barks, HarperOne, 2002
Sonia Shah, *Crude: The Story of Oil*, Seven Stories Press, 2004
Jeff VanderMeer, *Annihilation*, FSG Originals, 2014
Raúl Zurita, *Dreams for Kurosawa*, translated by Anna Deeny, arrow as aarow, 2012

I would like to especially single out *Annihilation* by Jeff VanderMeer and *Heart of Darkness* by Joseph Conrad as primary inspirations for the lighthouse sequence, and *The Crystal Text* by Clark Coolidge as inspiration for the figure of the second sun within that sequence.

The reference to the Persian term, *hezar-tu*, can be traced to the following text:

Somaiyeh Falahat, *Cities and Metaphors: Beyond Imaginaries of Islamic Urban Space*, Routledge, 2018

Acknowledgements

Thank you Matilda Fraser, Hera Lindsay Bird, Juliet Carpenter, Kim Pieters and Kim Wheatley for being my primary sources of validation and feedback throughout the process of writing this book. Thank you to the Grimshaw Sargeson Fellowship for the time, space and funds granted to me in 2017, during which time the bulk of this book was drafted. Thank you to the editors of hard press, Owen Connors and Anna Rankin, for spending time with me on a smaller iteration of the book. Thank you to Louisa Kasza and the rest of the team at Auckland University Press for enabling this book.

This book is dedicated to my partner, Tilly. Thank you for all your love and support. I could not have done this without you.

First published 2019
Auckland University Press
University of Auckland
Private Bag 92019
Auckland 1142
New Zealand
www.press.auckland.ac.nz

ISBN 978 1 86940 891 6

Published with the assistance of Creative New Zealand

A catalogue record for this book is available from
the National Library of New Zealand

Book design by Katrina Duncan
Cover design by Greg Simpson

Printed in Singapore by Markono Print Media Pte Ltd